INGMAR BERGMAN

Born in Sweden in 1918, Berg
screenwriter on *Frenzy* (Alf Sjöberg, 1944), but his
breakthrough as a director came in 1957 with both *The Seventh Seal*, in which a medieval knight (Max von Sydow) famously plays chess with Death, and *Wild Strawberries*. There followed in the sixties a trilogy of films each exploring existential doubt: *Through a Glass Darkly* (1961), *Winter Light* (1962) and *The Silence* (1963), as well as *The Virgin Spring*, and *Persona*. In the seventies he moved into television, most notably with *Scenes from a Marriage*, and in the eighties he returned to Sweden after working abroad to direct the popular, autobiographical film, *Fanny and Alexander*. Bergman was as active in the theatre as he was in film, working with many of the same company of actors. He was director of the theatre in Malmö (1953–60), of the Royal Dramatic Theatre in Stockholm (1960–6), and of the Residenztheater in Munich (1977–84). Three of his films, including *Through a Glass Darkly*, won Oscars for Best Foreign Language Film, and six were nominated for Best Original Screenplay, again including *Through a Glass Darkly*. Ingmar Bergman died in 2007.

JENNY WORTON

Jenny is Artistic Associate at the Almeida Theatre, London. She was previously the Literary Manager at the Tricycle Theatre, and worked in the Literary Departments for the Bush Theatre, the National Theatre and Out of Joint Theatre Company. She adapted *Dolls* (National Theatre of Scotland and Hush Productions) for the stage and acted as dramaturg for the Gate Theatre, London, on *Breathing Irregular*. She wrote the text for South Bank Show Award-nominated *I Am Falling* (the Gate and Sadler's Wells). Her original work for BBC Radio 4 includes *Demonstrating Grace* and *A Hallowed Space*.

Other Titles from Nick Hern Books

Jez Butterworth
JERUSALEM
MOJO
THE NIGHT HERON
PARLOUR SONG
THE WINTERLING

Caryl Churchill
BLUE HEART
CHURCHILL PLAYS: THREE
CHURCHILL PLAYS: FOUR
CHURCHILL: SHORTS
CLOUD NINE
A DREAM PLAY *after* Strindberg
DRUNK ENOUGH TO SAY I LOVE YOU?
FAR AWAY
HOTEL
ICECREAM
LIGHT SHINING IN BUCKINGHAMSHIRE
MAD FOREST
A NUMBER
SEVEN JEWISH CHILDREN
THE SKRIKER
THIS IS A CHAIR
THYESTES *after* Seneca
TRAPS

Ariel Dorfman
DEATH AND THE MAIDEN
PURGATORIO
READER
THE RESISTANCE TRILOGY
WIDOWS

David Edgar
ALBERT SPEER
ARTHUR & GEORGE *after* Julian Barnes
CONTINENTAL DIVIDE
DR JEKYLL AND MR HYDE *after* R.L. Stevenson
EDGAR: SHORTS
PENTECOST
PLAYING WITH FIRE
THE PRISONER'S DILEMMA
THE SHAPE OF THE TABLE
TESTING THE ECHO
A TIME TO KEEP *with* Stephanie Dale

Debbie Tucker Green
BORN BAD
DIRTY BUTTERFLY
RANDOM
STONING MARY
TRADE & GENERATIONS

Ayub Khan-Din
EAST IS EAST
LAST DANCE AT DUM DUM
NOTES ON FALLING LEAVES
RAFTA, RAFTA...

Tony Kushner
ANGELS IN AMERICA – PARTS ONE & TWO
CAROLINE, OR CHANGE
HOMEBODY/KABUL

Liz Lochhead
BLOOD AND ICE
DRACULA *after* Bram Stoker
EDUCATING AGNES ('The School for Wives') *after* Molière
GOOD THINGS
MEDEA *after* Euripides
MISERYGUTS & TARTUFFE *after* Molière
PERFECT DAYS
THEBANS

Conor McPherson
DUBLIN CAROL
McPHERSON: FOUR PLAYS
McPHERSON PLAYS: TWO
PORT AUTHORITY
THE SEAFARER
SHINING CITY
THE WEIR

Enda Walsh
BEDBOUND & MISTERMAN
DELIRIUM
DISCO PIGS & SUCKING DUBLIN
THE NEW ELECTRIC BALLROOM
THE SMALL THINGS
THE WALWORTH FARCE

Steve Waters
THE CONTINGENCY PLAN
FAST LABOUR
THE UNTHINKABLE
WORLD MUSIC

Ingmar Bergman

THROUGH A GLASS DARKLY

adapted for the stage by
Jenny Worton

NICK HERN BOOKS
London
www.nickhernbooks.co.uk

A Nick Hern Book

This dramatisation of *Through a Glass Darkly* first published in Great Britain in 2010 by Nick Hern Books, 14 Larden Road, London W3 7ST

Cover image: Ruth Wilson as Karin; photograph by Hugo Glendinning
Cover design: Ned Hoste, 2H

Typeset by Nick Hern Books, London
Printed in the UK by CLE Print Ltd, St Ives, Cambs, PE27 3LE

A CIP catalogue record for this book is available from the British Library

ISBN 978 1 84842 123 3

Through a Glass Darkly received its world premiere on stage at the Almeida Theatre, London, on 10 June 2010, in association with Andrew Higgie and Back Row Productions. The cast was as follows:

KARIN	Ruth Wilson
MARTIN	Justin Salinger
DAVID	Ian McElhinney
MAX	Dimitri Leonidas

Director	Michael Attenborough
Design	Tom Scutt
Lighting	Colin Grenfell
Music and Sound	Dan Jones
Assistant Director	Kate Hewitt

Characters

KARIN, *early to mid-twenties*
MARTIN, *early forties, Karin's husband*
DAVID, *fifty-eight, Karin and Max's father*
MAX, *sixteen, Karin's younger brother*

Setting

The play is set on an island off the coast of Sweden, in the family's holiday home. The house is on a beach. It is 1960.

Notes

A dash (–) *indicates an interruption by another character*

An ellipsis (…) *indicates a sentence trailing off*

Thanks

Jenny Worton would like to thank Michael Attenborough, Andrew Higgie, Garry McQuinn and Andrew Upton.

This text went to press before the end of rehearsals and so may differ slightly from the play as performed.

Scene One

From deep in the darkness at the back of the stage we hear laughter, ever so slightly forced. Four figures emerge, each wet from the sea. All make their way to the front of the stage and stand there dripping, looking out. The laughter fades.

Silence.

DAVID. I'd forgotten how beautiful the water was.

MAX. You say that every year.

KARIN. And every year he's right. This is the most wonderful place on earth. Isn't it, Dad?

DAVID. If you say so, darling.

MARTIN. She does, believe me, frequently.

KARIN. And I say that everything will be perfect this holiday.

MAX. Ha!

DAVID. Do you now?

KARIN. I do.

(*To* MARTIN.) You and Dad can put out the nets and Maxie and I will get started on dinner.

MARTIN. I think Max should help David with the nets so I can take a stroll with my wife.

DAVID. Or Maxie and Martin start dinner and Karin and I –

MAX. I've no intention of chopping vegetables or putting out the nets. I'll decide for myself what I'm going to do.

KARIN (*to* MARTIN *and* DAVID). Now look what you've done. You should have listened to me in the first place.

DAVID. Arbitration! The father will decide. Come on, Martin, let the children go inside, we hunters shall contend with the wind and the waves.

(*To* KARIN *and* MAX.) Go on, you'll catch your death out here.

KARIN. Brilliant plan, I wish I'd thought of it.

KARIN *drags* MAX *away.*

Come on, I want to get clean and dry.

MAX. I don't care about being clean.

They are gone.

DAVID. Shall we grab a jumper or just brave it?

MARTIN. What do you think?

DAVID. There's a wind up.

MARTIN. Really?

DAVID. I'm fine, but –

MARTIN. If you're cold we should…

DAVID. No. Not a bit. Are you okay?

MARTIN. I'm used to it. It's quite a breeze.

DAVID. What does not kill me makes me stronger and all that.

MARTIN. Hemingway eat your heart out, eh?

DAVID *begins gathering the nets to take out and* MARTIN *puts on a pair of shoes.*

DAVID. Storm clouds, do you think?

MARTIN. They won't reach us tonight. Afraid of a thunderstorm?

DAVID. You have no idea. The lack of control. You should see them tumbling out of the Alps.

MARTIN. How was Switzerland, aside from the storms?

DAVID. Brilliant.

MARTIN. So you enjoyed yourself?

DAVID. It wasn't pleasure, it was work. I missed you all. But I had to stay there and finish this damn book – I swore I would. Homesick or not.

MARTIN. And did you?

DAVID. What?

MARTIN. Finish it?

DAVID. More or less.

MARTIN. And your ulcer?

DAVID. All right. I might get you to prescribe something. I'll take the boat to town tomorrow.

MARTIN. I thought you were planning to spend the day here with us tomorrow?

DAVID. There are a few things I'm going to need to do.

MARTIN. I see.

DAVID. I can't pretend I don't exist because I'm on holiday with my family.

MARTIN. I know that.

DAVID. I exist, Martin, I have obligations.

MARTIN. We all know that.

Pause.

Just…

DAVID. Just what?

MARTIN. Just… know how much this holiday means to Karin. She's been planning for it for months.

DAVID. Planning for it? We do the same thing every year.

MARTIN. God only knows what she's been doing, other than talking about it constantly.

They have the nets and DAVID *turns to leave.* MARTIN *glances anxiously towards the house to make sure they aren't overheard.*

Did you get my last letter? I posted it weeks ago.

DAVID. I was incommunicado. Concentrating. You've got to work. I'm sixty in a couple of years.

MARTIN *is silent.*

I was in Zurich on Monday, and I flew home on Wednesday and then came straight here.

MARTIN. So you didn't get it?

DAVID. Is there something wrong?

MARTIN. Karin, it was an update on Karin.

DAVID. What about Karin?

MARTIN. About her health.

I felt I should keep you up to date, even if it interrupted your creative flow.

DAVID. Well?

MARTIN. When she came home from the hospital, a month ago now, I asked her psychiatrist what I should expect.

DAVID. Is that the letter you're talking about? I got that one.

MARTIN. No, not the first one. This was an update.

DAVID. I got the letter about her stay in hospital.

MARTIN. I know.

DAVID. I was in the thick of it at the time. I couldn't –

MARTIN. So was she.

DAVID. I got that letter… a while ago.

MARTIN. This was a different letter: an update after she left hospital.

The psychiatrist, this is a man I trust, said he couldn't promise there wouldn't be a relapse.

Silence.

DAVID. How's it been over the last month?

MARTIN. She responded well in hospital so she's off the drugs now. Her hearing is oversensitive and she hasn't much of an appetite. I have noticed she doesn't want to see anyone, none of our friends. She'd rather be alone most of the time. Hence the importance of this holiday.

And she doesn't sleep.

DAVID. Well, that could be said about any of us. Me, Maxie, it was true of Karin's mother too. I suppose if you're looking for symptoms…

You're just lucky, nothing disturbs your sleep!

MARTIN *remains silent.*

What does Karin know?

MARTIN. Everything, of course. Essentially. Well, she knows there could be a relapse. But not that it's likely to be persistent.

DAVID. Persistent?

MARTIN. The condition is probably chronic. There are cases of complete recovery, so there's always hope.

I don't think we need to upset her by telling her too much.

DAVID. No. It didn't help her mother.

MARTIN. You told her?

DAVID. I told her what the doctors told me.

MARTIN. And?

DAVID. It terrified her. The knowledge.

Ultimately, I've always believed, that it led to her death.

Quiet.

Look, the book is nearly finished, I made sure of that. I want to give Karin some time. Both of them. This summer.

And you, of course.

How are you keeping?

MARTIN. Not so bad.

DAVID. That's a short answer.

MARTIN. I assumed you were being polite.

DAVID *laughs*.

DAVID. Am I that bad?

MARTIN. It's been hard. The days pass. Never enough time. I moved my practice, got myself a bit more space, I think I said all that in the letter.

DAVID. The missing letter?

MARTIN. No. The one you got.

DAVID. How's Maxie? Do you think? He seems all right.

MARTIN. He's got his own troubles.

DAVID. Has he?

MARTIN. Well, yes, certainly. He's a teenager. I don't know.

Before the illness, we were happy. I mean it, Karin and I were happy. What scared me was how bad it had got, by the time I realised she'd already been through so much.

DAVID. Yes. I remember you saying in one of your letters.

MARTIN. I didn't tell you the half of it. You were so busy with your novel. I didn't want to upset you.

What I'm saying is that I've come to understand through all this how much I love her. And I'm all she has to cling to in life, the only thing she can rely on.

DAVID. I see.

MARTIN. She says to me I'm her only defence against the disease. And she's right. I think our happiness in being together is the best cure.

Silence.

I just wanted you to know.

DAVID (*about the nets*). We should put these out.

Scene Two

Inside the house we can see KARIN*'s naked back. She is drying herself off with a towel after washing.*

MAX *is revealed standing there watching her.* KARIN *finally notices him, bundles up her towel and flicks it at him playfully.*

KARIN. There you are. Aren't you going to wash?

She throws the towel at him and disappears off to finish dressing.

MAX. I like the salt in my hair. I like the feeling of the sea drying on my skin.

I didn't wash my hair all summer once. Do you remember? It was before Martin. You might even have still been at school. The whole summer I went around with my hair caked in salt and sand. I could taste it on my fingers after I scratched my head.

KARIN (*offstage*). Disgusting.

MAX. I washed. Every now and then.

KARIN *returns, dressed.*

KARIN. Still disgusting.

MAX. I just didn't wash my hair. It's not disgusting.

KARIN. What's that stench?

He flicks the towel, which he has kept hold of, at her. She grabs it and a tug of war ensues.

What is that awful stink?

MAX. It must be you – it's your towel.

She catches him off guard and gives a big pull, he loses his balance and falls into her. MAX *pulls away quickly.*

KARIN. What is it?

What's the matter?

MAX. The walls in this place are so thin; I can't help hearing you and Martin talking and scratching away at each other. You're always at it... sex, I reckon.

Can't you keep it to yourselves? And the door, you should shut the door to your room. So that we can all, you know, just live. Privacy basically. Let everyone else just get on with it.

KARIN. Maxie.

MAX. Stay away from me. You'd better watch out. I mean it, Karin. You can't be hugging and kissing me all the time any more. And don't lie there half naked when you're sunbathing, it makes me feel sick to see you like that.

KARIN. What do you mean? Sick?

MAX. You know exactly what I mean.

Women! With all their smells and hair-brushing, their secret things! What am I meant to do?

You just standing there like that, drying yourself with the door wide open, I feel like I'm being skinned alive. The whole time.

KARIN. Oh Maxie, poor Maxie –

MAX. And, don't 'poor Maxie' me, it's always 'poor me, poor me'. Don't worry about me on the self-pity front. I can 'poor me' plenty on my own.

KARIN *snuggles up beside him, to hug him and calm him.*

Don't tell Dad any of this.

KARIN. Don't be silly.

MAX. You think I'm a joke?

He jumps to his feet.

I'm not a fucking joke.

KARIN. I know, I know.

He slumps.

Come on, let's go do the veg.

Grab the chairs, I'll meet you outside.

She pulls him out of the bedroom, and leads him outside. KARIN *begins peeling potatoes.*

What's bothering you so much?

MAX. If I could just once in my life talk to Dad. I know he would understand. But he's so involved in his own things.

KARIN. Tonight you'll be able to show him your play. That'll be good.

MAX. Maybe.

KARIN. Excited?

MAX *shrugs.*

Nervous?

MAX. No.

KARIN. It's wonderful that you and Daddy have got something in common now. I think this summer the two of you are going to come to understand each other. Like –

MAX. Frankenstein and his monster.

KARIN. What? No!

MAX. Do you want to go over it again?

MAX *takes some pages from his back pocket.*

KARIN. I think I've got it. I'm only doing the Prologue.

MAX. I know that, but it's about making sure –

KARIN. Yes, the rhythm, I know.

MAX. Otherwise, it won't make sense.

KARIN. I think I've got it, honestly. I'll make you proud.

MAX *puts the pages away again.*

He's going to love it.

MAX. I wouldn't get your hopes up, it's not a novel.

KARIN. So?

MAX. He'll think it's about him.

KARIN. Well, it isn't.

Is it?

I didn't think it was.

MAX. It's about art. He shouldn't assume just because he's a writer…

KARIN *suddenly looks worried.*

Oh, you don't understand.

Nobody understands.

This year's been awful.

KARIN. You've grown so much.

MAX. Great.

What an incredible achievement.

KARIN. What about Dad?

MAX. What about him?

KARIN. Are you pleased to see him? I am.

MAX. Yeah. As long as he doesn't... You know, he's so...

KARIN. Don't.

MAX. What?

KARIN. Nothing.

Do you think he seems happy?

MAX. Happy?

I thought more tired really, from all the travelling.

KARIN. Maybe.

MAX. What shouldn't I do?

KARIN. You know.

MAX. No.

KARIN. You know what Dad's like. Don't make a fuss all the time. Don't ask for too much. Try to be flexible.

Quiet.

MAX. I didn't think he looked that happy really.

KARIN. Marianne?

MAX. Yeah.

KARIN. Poor Dad.

All alone again.

MAX. I didn't like Marianne.

KARIN. She was very sure of herself, wasn't she? Everything was 'do this, do that'. Dad seemed quite simple and straightforward by comparison.

I don't know why he can't just find someone more like Mummy.

MAX. She was rude about his books. She undermined him.

KARIN. Mummy?

MAX. Marianne!

He's got to succeed with this book. He has to get good reviews.

KARIN. Everyone reads his books.

MAX. That's not the point. He doesn't care how many copies he sells. He wants to be praised critically. I know. He wants to be seen as a genius, that's what matters to him.

KARIN *laughs suddenly.*

What?

KARIN. Listen to you –

MAX. What's so funny?

KARIN. So serious. 'He must be seen as a genius, that's what matters to him.'

MAX. Jesus.

She laughs again.

KARIN. I'm only teasing.

She hugs him.

Oh, I'm sorry, you know I love you and how serious everything is for you. I do understand.

It's drastic how grown-up you are.

MAX. What are you going on about?

KARIN. My little brother, sixteen years old and already the tortured artist. I bet the girls love it! I bet you're beating them off with a stick.

MAX. Stop it. If you're going to talk like an idiot you can do this on your own.

KARIN. Come on.

Everything can't always be about Dad. That's all I meant. Let's talk about you.

MAX. Me?

KARIN. Have you got a girlfriend?

MAX. Who'd want to go out with me?

KARIN. Oh, I don't know, there's something trustworthy about you. Something gentle and kind.

MAX. Very sexy: the great friend.

KARIN. I'm sorry I laughed at you.

Forgive me? Please?

She kisses him lightly.

MAX. You don't have to apologise. There's nothing to apologise for: I am ridiculous. I know I'm ridiculous. It's good for me to be laughed at.

KARIN. I think Dad has written some lovely books.

MAX. But not great books.

He's not a genius. And never will be, no matter how hard he works. And that's –

KARIN. Quiet!

MAX. What?

KARIN. Did you hear that call?

MAX. No.

KARIN. It was a storm petrel. Yes. Now. You must hear it.

MAX. Still can't.

KARIN. It's odd, but since the hospital my hearing has become so sensitive. Sudden loud noises scare the life out of me.

KARIN *looks around.*

MAX. What's the matter?

KARIN. Nothing. Nothing.

MAX. Are you all right?

KARIN. Do you sometimes think birds are sort of terrifying?

MAX. Birds?

KARIN. Because they're above everything, they see what we're doing down here.

MAX. I don't think the birds care what you're doing.

KARIN. Don't be scared. Everything is going to be fine.

MAX. I'm not scared.

As KARIN *remains seated, the following scene emerges around her.*

Scene Three

The table is littered with the remains of dinner: a pot of fish stew, an empty bottle of wine. Everyone is sitting at the table.

KARIN. You're a master chef, Dad.

DAVID. Darling, you hardly ate.

MARTIN. That was fantastic.

MAX. Maybe you should write cookery books instead of novels.

Everybody laughs, a shade too brightly.

MARTIN. Well, here's to the chef. And welcome back, David.

They all toast and drink.

KARIN. Welcome back to our holiday island paradise.

DAVID. Reminds me of when you were little, being here.

KARIN. With Mummy?

DAVID. Yes.

KARIN (*to* MAX). Us going off on one of our adventures. Remember?

MAX. Not really.

KARIN (*to* MARTIN). Mummy used to make up these incredible games to stop us getting bored during the summer. She was so much fun, you would have loved her.

Silence.

DAVID. Anyway, when we're here I always think of the two of you as children. And me as the young strong father!

MAX. Except Martin's not quite Mummy.

Silence.

DAVID. The novel's really coming along, you know. Really. I'm still amazed at how hard it is, after all these years. Confronting the silence inside.

After forty years, there's never an easy day.

Not made any easier by being away, of course. If you only knew how I've been longing for this moment.

MAX. You've been longing for this moment?

DAVID. I was homesick every minute I was away.

MAX. Homesick? For us?

DAVID. Maybe not for you.

MARTIN. You missed Karin and Max?

DAVID. I did.

KARIN. We missed you.

MAX. And are you going to stay put now?

DAVID. I'm looking forward to going mushrooming with my daughter.

Such a beautiful night. You forget this. This clear, simple air and the sound of the sea.

Quiet.

Last year of school?

MAX. Coming up.

DAVID. Looking forward to it?

MAX. Will you be at home?

DAVID. Excited?

MAX. Yeah.

DAVID. Your whole life ahead of you. I'm almost envious.

MAX. Will you be at home with me after the holidays?

DAVID. Of course. As much as I can be.

MAX. How much is that?

DAVID. Like I say, as much as I can.

MAX. I'm just asking.

DAVID. I'm with you all summer.

KARIN. What? You aren't going away again this year?

DAVID. Let's just take it a step at a time.

KARIN. But it's Maxie's –

MARTIN. He means a short trip. Don't you, David?

DAVID. Well. You know… I'm sure I told you all this?

I'm lecturing in Yugoslavia. It'll be a –

KARIN. Yugoslavia? But what for? Why?

DAVID. It's part of a literature course.

They're studying a couple of my novels. It's a very flattering offer, and it helps the university. I know the country well, so…

MARTIN. It sounds quite important. But short?

MAX. What about your book?

DAVID (*to* MARTIN*'s question*). Yes. A term.

(*To* MAX.) My book? You know, that's, that's got to be finished and at the publishers' by then. I'm going to get it off by the end of next week. That's my plan. While I'm here.

MAX. How long will you be away?

DAVID. As Martin says, it's short.

Dubrovnik is a wonderful city, I haven't spent any time there for years…

They are very responsive to my work there.

Which…

The conversation peters into silence. DAVID *looks from one to the other, then laughs.*

What is this? All of a sudden I feel like the bad guy.

MAX. You promised you'd stay at home after this novel.

DAVID. I'm here. On holiday. Here I am. And you're back at boarding school in the autumn, so…

I promised?

I know we talked about it. Did I promise? I can't have foreseen this, you see, it's a real honour.

I don't remember promising.

MAX. You promised.

DAVID. What I would have meant. By a promise like that. I would have meant. Ideally. If I can. But I can't, you see?

MAX. I see.

DAVID. Do you? Do you understand?

Silence.

KARIN. We were going to have such fun this evening and now we're nearly crying.

DAVID *laughs quickly.*

DAVID. No. Look. I'm here now. Here I am.

And, and look before I forget, I brought you all presents from Switzerland.

From a bag under the table he hands out a wrapped present to each of them, then looks around quickly as if for help, he stands suddenly.

I'll just get my tobacco.

As DAVID *heads off to the house* KARIN, MAX *and* MARTIN *sit in silence.*

MARTIN. What did you get?

The three begin to unwrap their presents.

Above them, DAVID *is hunting for his tobacco.*

KARIN. A pair of gloves.

MAX. Another watch.

MARTIN. An electric razor.

DAVID *stops his hunting breathlessly, as if at a loss. He begins to sob dryly, takes a deep breath but only cries more violently, bashing his fists into his forehead in an attempt to suppress the despair that is overwhelming him. Finally he controls himself, gathers up his tobacco and tidies himself up.*

MAX. I bet he didn't think to buy these till he was at the airport.

KARIN (*about the gloves*). They're a bit small.

MARTIN. It's the thought that counts.

MAX. I'd rather have the money.

DAVID *returns and the three spring up to thank him for their presents.*

DAVID. Here we are then.

MARTIN. Thank you.

MAX. Thanks.

DAVID. How're the gloves? I thought of your hands.

KARIN. They'll be lovely.

DAVID. I thought the watch might come in handy with your exams next year.

I really didn't know what to get you. To surprise you.

KARIN. Maxie has got a surprise for you too.

MAX. No, Karin.

DAVID. Really? What?

MAX. It's nothing.

KARIN. Go on, give it to him.

MAX. It doesn't matter.

DAVID. I'd like a surprise.

KARIN. That's right. (*To* MAX.) You've been working so hard.

DAVID. This is exciting.

KARIN. It is.

MAX (*at length*). All right then.

MAX *takes the handful of papers from his back pocket and places them in front of* DAVID *on the table.*

It's a play.

KARIN. It's theatre.

MAX. I wrote it.

KARIN (*to* DAVID). He wants your opinion, don't you?

MAX. Of course.

DAVID *stares at the play but does not move to pick it up.*

DAVID. Yes. This is very exciting, Maxie.

MAX. Not really.

KARIN. Just to whet your appetite, I'm going to perform the Prologue. And then you can savour the rest when you have time.

I've read it, it's excellent, but he doesn't care what I think.

MARTIN. I've not read it.

MAX. Shut up, Karin.

MARTIN. He wouldn't let me.

DAVID. I didn't know you were writing.

When did you start writing?

MAX *shrugs.*

KARIN. Two writers in the family now.

You two, you're like…

She glances at MAX.

Peas in a pod.

You'll like it, Dad, it's about art.

DAVID (*reading from but not touching the paper*). '*The Artist and Death.*'

KARIN *gets up, gathers the pages and stands in front of the table. She smiles.*

KARIN. '*The Artist and Death –* '

DAVID. That's all right, darling, I'd like to read it later, when I can really give it my full attention.

There is a brief silence while everyone takes this in.

KARIN. Are you sure? I was just going to do the Prologue.

DAVID. Well, exactly, I'd like to read the whole thing.

KARIN. Right, yes – (*Glancing at* MAX.) but you must remember that the rhythm is terribly important. When you read it.

DAVID. Of course.

MARTIN. We could all read it now, together, do the voices.

MAX *and* DAVID. No!

MAX. No, later. Dad can read it later.

DAVID. Yes, great, I'll look forward to that.

KARIN *offers* DAVID *the play, but he has stood up and is gathering dishes.*

Just leave it on the table, will you.

Who's going to help me with the dishes, then?

MARTIN *and* KARIN *linger a little and then help* DAVID. MAX *just watches.*

MARTIN. What's on tomorrow? Into town?

KARIN. I thought we were staying here, spending some time together, just the four of us.

MARTIN. David says we need supplies. We could all go.

DAVID. I might go to town. You should all stay here, catch up.

DAVID *exits with the dishes.* MAX*'s play remains on the table. He stares at it and then runs off.*

KARIN. Maxie!

But he has disappeared. KARIN *starts to follow.*

MARTIN. Where are you going?

KARIN. To find Maxie.

MARTIN. Come to bed.

KARIN. Can't you see what's happened? He's devastated.

MARTIN. It's fine.

Don't worry so much. You can't fix everything.

But KARIN *is staring out, not listening to* MARTIN.

Where have you gone?

KARIN. I knew it was all going to go to pieces. That stupid bird!

MARTIN. Karin?

KARIN. What?

What are you talking about?

You look so anxious.

MARTIN. I'm not anxious.

KARIN. Always so anxious about me.

MARTIN. I want you to know I'm here for you. My dear little girl.

He turns her to him. She avoids his gaze at first but then looks at him.

KARIN. 'My little girl.' You love that: me being little. Am I a girl or is it that my… illness has made me a child?

Am I ill? Or am I odd? Backwards perhaps?

MARTIN. You know the answer to that.

KARIN. Do I? Of course.

MARTIN. Do you believe me?

KARIN. Yes. I don't know.

MARTIN. Well, you must know.

That's marriage. And through that, by seeing ourselves through others, that's how we make reality. And that's how we can be secure.

And you've gone again.

KARIN. What?

MARTIN. Where do you go? When you drift away from me.

KARIN. Nowhere.

KARIN *staring out.*

MARTIN. Don't you believe I love you?

KARIN. Yes. I believe it.

MARTIN. Is it enough?

It used to be?

Remember?

KARIN. Yes. Of course it's enough.

She sighs, suddenly, deeply, tragically miserable.

Oh Martin.

MARTIN. Come to bed.

KARIN. What about Dad? Why was he so ungenerous about the play? Maxie was upset. What a mess. What a mess.

MARTIN. Bed.

Scene Four

And the bed is there. KARIN *looks around the room.* MARTIN *is in the bathroom.*

KARIN. Are you tired? I'm not tired at all.

MARTIN *sticks his head round the door, mouth full of toothpaste.*

MARTIN. What?

She does not respond. He disappears again with his pyjamas in his hand. KARIN *goes to the cupboard, opens it and lifts her nightdress out. She stops and smells her nightdress, it smells bad. She leans down into the cupboard and sniffs: the cupboard smells. She lifts the pile of clothes out and then looks around the room. She sees the drawer under the bed and walks over to it. She opens it and starts to rearrange* MARTIN*'s things so she can fit her clothes in. As she does so she suddenly sees something that upsets her. She hesitates for a moment, looks to the bathroom and then closes the drawer. She takes her pile of clothes back to the cupboard and puts them inside.*

MARTIN *comes into the bedroom in his pyjamas.* KARIN *begins to undress.*

Fresh fish, nothing quite like it!

He is watching her undress. She turns her back to him to change. They move to either side of the bed. KARIN *hesitates,* MARTIN *hesitates, they stand facing each other.*

Are you okay?

KARIN. Are you?

MARTIN. Yes.

He goes to get in.

What is it, darling?

KARIN. Are you tired? I'm not tired at all.

Why are we tired if we rest all day?

MARTIN. I took a long swim this morning.

What's wrong?

Sudden.

KARIN. Can I share your drawer?

MARTIN. What?

KARIN. I'm looking for a place to put my clothes.

MARTIN. You have a cupboard.

KARIN. It smells.

MARTIN. Does it?

KARIN *remains silent, challenging.*

If you want.

He goes to the drawer and is trying to manage it privately. She is at his shoulder.

KARIN. The cupboard is very musty, it smells bad.

He stops trying to organise. He turns to her. She is angling to see inside the drawer.

MARTIN. Is it? Okay –

KARIN. It's making all my clothes stink.

MARTIN. Right.

He is blocking her.

KARIN. It is. I'm not making it up as an excuse to look in…

I wasn't poking around.

MARTIN. What? Karin? What is it?

KARIN. I was just looking to clear a bit of space for my things.

They're hidden there at the back, underneath your shirts.

MARTIN. What are you talking about?

KARIN. Sedatives. Syringes.

Sedatives. Needles. Syringes.

MARTIN. I'm a doctor.

KARIN. Yes, I know that.

MARTIN. So?

KARIN. Why did you bring those?

MARTIN. I'm a doctor. I didn't think about it.

It's part of my daily… Did you bring sanitary towels?

And your period isn't due?

KARIN. It will be.

MARTIN. You know what I mean.

KARIN. Martin –

MARTIN. What were you doing poking around in my drawer?

KARIN. You're obviously…

I wasn't poking around in your drawer.

MARTIN. What?

Obviously what?

KARIN. I wasn't poking around in your drawer, I needed some space.

MARTIN. I'll have the cupboard.

KARIN. We can share. That's not the point. What I'm saying. What I'm really asking…

I need you to tell me. I need to know.

MARTIN. Look, listen to me, I didn't bring my medical supplies for any reason other than I didn't think about it.

KARIN. I'm sorry, I wasn't poking around. Are you hiding something from me?

You would tell me, wouldn't you?

Whatever you're planning.

MARTIN. I'm not planning anything. Darling, look at me, the best way for you to get better, the only way for you to get better, is not to let yourself get anxious and feed this silly paranoia. Really. Look at me, I brought my supplies because quite frankly… I didn't think about it.

He is guiding her away from the drawer.

I want you to swim, rest, read, enjoy your family and me, enjoy our love for each other and don't drift away from us. Then I promise you will get better. Okay?

That's how it works. Just enjoy doing the things that everyone does and that's how you get better. Act like everyone else. And before you know it, you'll be like everyone else. It's very simple.

KARIN. I wasn't poking around.

MARTIN. I didn't say you were.

KARIN. All the time I was growing up I never wanted to be a burden to my father and now look at me.

MARTIN. I want you to trust me. You need to trust that you and I want the same thing. I've seen how you suffer. All I want is for you to be well.

Quiet.

KARIN. I'm not even worried about all that.

I just want Dad to be happy and I want Maxie to be happy.

I think we can solve it. Get them to talk to each other.

MARTIN. We can. We can. Sleep for one thing will do it. Come on, darling. We'll sleep it all away.

He begins to tuck her into bed. It becomes apparent that this is a ritual, like a father with a child. He straightens the bedclothes around her and organises her arms and hands above the covers as he speaks. He strokes her, tucks her hair behind her ears. KARIN *submits to all this.*

Tomorrow morning will be sunny and we'll go for a swim. You're going to have a lovely holiday, surrounded by the people you love.

KARIN. Holidays! They're supposed to be relaxing but in fact they're just lumps of time without any distractions.

We spend our whole lives turning our faces away and then we have all this time and we… I find myself staring into the abyss.

MARTIN. What?

KARIN. Nothing.

I hope I didn't upset you, I'm only worrying about my family.

Sometimes I think the only thing Maxie and I have ever really talked about is Dad. He's our obsession.

Forgive me.

MARTIN. There's nothing to forgive. You can't upset me. I love you.

KARIN. You're so kind and I am so nasty.

Poor Dad, we scare him to death.

MARTIN. Be quiet now.

KARIN *nods.* MARTIN*'s stroking becomes sexual.* KARIN *remains still, tense, confined by the blankets he has wrapped her in.* KARIN *suddenly huddles into herself and moves away from* MARTIN. *He looks hurt, but quietly lies down next to her.*

Scene Five

Time passes. It's four in the morning. Distant sounds of a horn on a ship. MARTIN *is asleep but* KARIN *is restless. The noise of the seagulls is scaring her. She hears whispering. She gets up and tiptoes out, drawn to another room in the house. The room is derelict, the walls are covered in faded wallpaper. There is a large crack in one wall, which* KARIN *moves towards. The whispering intensifies.*

KARIN *concentrates, listening, her whole body attentive. Gradually, she sighs, breathes deeply and smiles gratefully. She begins to whisper in response to what she has heard. Her words may only be partly audible but what she says is: 'I want to, I'm trying, please wait for me. It's such a comfort to know you're all there.'*

KARIN *is quiet again. Her eyes glaze over and she sinks to her knees. She holds onto herself tightly. There is something both sexual and deeply devotional in the way she holds her body.*

Scene Six

DAVID *has been up all night working on his manuscript.*

DAVID (*reads*). 'The desolate beach stretched out around them. She came toward him, panting with expectation, her face reddened in the keen wind…' Oh my God, oh my God.

He gives up and then tries again.

'She came toward him, panting with expectation.'

He runs a line through the manuscript.

She came running toward him, her face reddened in the keen wind.

She came toward him. She hurried along.

There is hurry. Hurry and rush.

He laughs derisively. He picks up his pen and scores at the manuscript.

DAVID *moves away from the desk and goes to the mirror.*

She was pleased to see him. It never crossed her mind the clichéd convenience of it all, taking place on a windswept beach. The achingly obvious poetry of the ocean and the artfully barren stretch of fucking coast!

You idiot. You oaf. You donkey. You clumsy fuck.

He hits himself. And again and again.

You coward.

He turns away from the mirror, KARIN *is in the room behind him.*

KARIN. Dad?

DAVID. Jesus Christ. Karin. Sorry.

I couldn't sleep.

KARIN. The muse has called?

DAVID. Finishing up for the publisher.

KARIN. Read it to me? Is it good?

He shakes his head to say no.

DAVID. It's okay.

You need your sleep. Why aren't you asleep?

KARIN. The birds.

At sunrise they make such a noise. You can almost hear them eating, clacking their beaks.

And then I think about their eyes. The way they're yellow. It scares me and I can't go back to sleep.

What were you doing?

DAVID. Finishing touches.

KARIN. You were hitting yourself.

DAVID. Keeping myself awake. You have to keep yourself awake and alert all the time.

I'm sorry.

Four a.m. It's not a very easy time of day. For me.

I want to write. So much. When you read one of those books, you know, great works, books that somehow dig inside you and reveal everything. Like someone's broken into you.

I have written, published, twelve novels.

A book of essays.

A handful of poems. Published poems.

I haven't written anything.

But I could. It's there. I feel this story in me.

He taps his chest.

There's something inside. There are times still when I can feel it burning inside me. But as I get older it wavers. Oh God, there are times, terrible times when I see my life laid out before me. And away to the side there is this other thing, this thing I was meant to write.

No. We all settle for something in the end.

KARIN. Don't settle. You have to follow your calling. No matter how hard it may seem, you must make difficult choices.

DAVID *starts to tidy his manuscript away.*

DAVID. You must.

KARIN. When there is something you know for certain.

It's the same for me. I'm beginning to think that I have a calling.

DAVID. Yes.

KARIN. We understand each other.

You understand, don't you?

DAVID. Well… as much as I can.

KARIN. But Martin, on the other hand, he's –

DAVID. He means well. But he is a bit holier-than-thou.

KARIN. He's not holy. At all.

DAVID. Well, who is?

KARIN *touches his hand; she wants to explain something to him.*

KARIN. Dad –

DAVID. Well, yes, you.

KARIN. Dad, I think something important is happening –

DAVID. No more for now, Karin. We've talked enough. You need your sleep, angel.

KARIN *pauses as if she might challenge him, but she does not.*

KARIN. Read to me?

DAVID. Not now. I have work to do. You should rest.

KARIN. I am tired.

DAVID. It's early yet. You can go back to sleep. Everything will be all right.

DAVID *guides* KARIN *over to the bed and tucks her in.*

KARIN. Do be kind to Maxie.

DAVID. I don't know why you say that.

KARIN. I know how much you want it to be right –

DAVID. Of course.

KARIN. But it goes wrong when you try.

Doesn't it?

DAVID *is silent.*

It's okay, you know. It's his age. Everything is so raw for him.

DAVID. And what about you? What about your age? What age are you? So worried about all of us.

He leans down and strokes her hair.

KARIN. Just like being little again.

He sits at the edge of the bed. KARIN *relaxes and falls asleep.*

DAVID *leaves the bed and sits back at the desk. He puts away the manuscript, disgusted. Underneath is* MAX*'s play, he picks it up and starts to read it, but he can't manage more than a few lines. He puts it down on the desk. Then turns it over. He puts his head in his hands.*

MAX *appears at the window.*

MAX. Dad.

DAVID *almost jumps out of his skin.*

DAVID. Jesus, Maxie!

MAX. The sun's coming up.

DAVID. You're like spectres, first Karin, now you, the pair of you. Scaring the living daylights out of me.

MAX. We could bring in the nets together.

DAVID. Shh, Karin's asleep.

MAX. Do you want to?

DAVID *thinks about it. He goes to collect his shoes. When his back is turned,* MAX *jumps in the window. He sees his play on* DAVID*'s desk, picks it up and tucks it into the back of his jeans.*

DAVID. Have you got shoes?

Where are your shoes?

MAX *is doing handstands.*

MAX. Last year it was as easy to walk on my hands as my feet.

He is back upright.

I'm too tall now to keep my balance. I feel unstable.

DAVID. You'll get used to it.

MAX. Were you writing tonight?

DAVID. Of course.

MAX. I'm like that. I've written six plays this summer and an opera.

DAVID. I find it better just to concentrate on one thing at a time.

MAX. But it just pours out. The writing's the easy bit. Don't you think?

DAVID. On a good night.

MAX. The one I gave you took an afternoon, basically. And then I kept polishing it. What did you think? Have you read it? That's what they're like.

DAVID. Honestly, I haven't had time yet.

MAX. That's the style of them.

You left it on the table.

DAVID. Look. It doesn't really matter what I think. It's about you.

MAX. I know that. I do know that. But it's hard, being an artist. We're not supposed to care what anyone thinks, we're supposed to stay in our towers. But actually we do obviously want people to like it. We want people to like us, don't we?

DAVID. Umm.

MAX. The one I gave you is about a writer and his muse. In it the muse is a woman, a temptress. She's all plump and sexy, but she's brutal to the writer! She keeps him caged and away from everything he loves, and occasionally she has sex with him.

DAVID. Right.

MAX. But that's a metaphor.

DAVID. I see.

MAX. For inspiration.

DAVID. Ah.

MAX. And in the end, the writer, he murders her!

DAVID. The muse?

MAX. Yeah, but it turns out after that she's actually really his wife.

Do you see?

DAVID *is silent.*

His art is responsible –

DAVID. I get it.

Are you serious about writing?

MAX. I do it a lot. It's good to talk about it because I haven't really talked to anyone about it before.

MAX *takes the play from his jeans and hands it to* DAVID *for a second time, it is not a challenge,* MAX *is vulnerable.* DAVID *pauses and then takes it.*

I like doing plays and dialogue. It's fun to experiment with style.

DAVID. Fun? There's your first mistake.

Style should never be confused with content. Style is an assistant to the act of communication. When it becomes an end in itself your reader feels cheated, like they have come all this way and only got to the secretary, not the man in charge.

MAX. You haven't even read it.

DAVID. I've learnt a thing or two over the years. You can't cheat, Maxie.

MAX *stares at his father and then grabs the play out of his hands.*

Maxie?

He is walking away.

DAVID. What about the nets?

MAX. You bring in the nets.

DAVID. Maxie?

MAX *comes back.*

MAX. You're so –

DAVID. You asked my opinion on writing.

You're acting like a child.

MAX. Fuck you.

He leaves.

DAVID. Maxie. Max?

You have to grow up. You need to face…

But he is gone.

…the real world.

DAVID *glances at* KARIN *in the bed, then follows* MAX *off.*

Scene Seven

Time passes. KARIN *climbs out of bed and is looking at everything on* DAVID*'s desk. She starts to go through his drawers. She finds* DAVID*'s diary.*

She reads it.

KARIN. 'Poor Karin. Martin has informed me that her illness is as bad as I feared: chronic in fact. And here I am all over again. I think of Ellen. I think of her terrifying certainty, delusions so wild and yet so convinced, so persuasive. I remember waking up and not being able to find her, Karin and Maxie gone from their beds. My desperation, my fury when she came back from her adventure. The children cold and tired. Thankfully, Karin does not really remember, does not know what is to come. And there are no children to worry for.

KARIN *is obviously reeling at this. She has to keep reading.*

I can't help thinking that was the closest I ever came to a real insight. That period around Ellen's decline was my most productive and driven. And I wonder, I do, face it, I do. There is a cold glimmer in my eye. That I might get a chance with age and experience to watch again the decline of a person. That Karin's illness is also a chance for me to see into the heart of madness and delusion. The sliver of ice in my writer's heart never ceases to surprise me.

Poor Karin, even so. Poor Karin, of course.'

KARIN *puts the diary away and leaves her father's room.*

She walks towards the derelict room in search of comfort. As she puts her hand on the door, she hears MARTIN *sleepily call her name. She freezes. Reluctantly,* KARIN *turns away and enters her own room.*

Scene Eight

MARTIN *is splayed across the bed. When he hears the door close, he murmurs her name again.* KARIN *is agitated. She crosses to the bed and leans over* MARTIN. *Her speech is rapid.*

KARIN. Martin! Martin! Wakey, wakey.

You're always asleep. The sun's up high in the sky. Martin!

MARTIN. What time is it?

KARIN. It's ten. It's nearly ten.

MARTIN. What? I've slept for hours!

He checks the time.

It isn't ten.

KARIN. Isn't it? It feels like it. I've been up having any number of adventures.

MARTIN. Give me a hug.

KARIN. Come on. We'll go for a swim, sleepyhead. Dad and Maxie are off somewhere. It's all go, go, go.

She kisses him suddenly and impulsively on the mouth. He tries to stay with the kiss but she slips away.

The only thing wrong with you as a member of our holy family is that you can sleep. That's the only way you don't quite make it into the very inner circle. You sleep and we are all total insomniacs. Sometimes Mummy wouldn't sleep for days and days. We'd do all these everyday things in the middle of the night, like cleaning and cooking. Once, when we were here, she took us to bring in the nets in the middle of the night. Mummy said it was the best time to go because the fish weren't expecting it and Maxie fell asleep standing up and fell and was hurt and Daddy was furious when we got back.

She laughs and then, remembering her father's diary, cries and buries herself in MARTIN*'s chest.*

MARTIN. Karin?

KARIN. Nothing. It's nothing. I'm such an idiot.

MARTIN. What is it, Karin?

KARIN. I can't talk about it.

MARTIN. Karin, please.

KARIN. No. It's impossible. Don't you see? I've always had it wrong. I haven't understood. I've been trying so hard to make us all a family –

MARTIN. We are a family.

KARIN. Not you. My family: me, Maxie, my father. It used to be fine before Mummy died and I have tried for so long –

MARTIN. It's not your responsibility –

KARIN. Don't you see, it was never fine, we were never fine.

MARTIN. I don't understand.

KARIN. I can't explain, they're not my words.

MARTIN. Words? Whose words?

KARIN. Until now, I haven't understood.

Daddy's.

In his diary.

MARTIN. You read David's diary?

She nods.

Oh, Karin.

KARIN. There was quite a lot in it about me.

MARTIN. I see. About your illness?

KARIN. Yes.

MARTIN. I told David you might possibly have a relapse. But you knew that.

KARIN. Yes.

And Mummy had what I have.

MARTIN. We can only speculate.

It's no more than that.

KARIN. Do you promise?

MARTIN. I promise.

KARIN. There was something else too.

MARTIN. What?

Perhaps David misunderstood.

KARIN. I can't tell you.

MARTIN. Please.

KARIN. Ask him yourself.

You'll have to ask him to tell you.

Come on, sleepyhead. It's a holiday.

She laughs and pulls him out of bed. MARTIN *can't keep up.*

We should swim. Cool, fresh water.

They kiss once. Then KARIN *breaks away again.*

Be patient with me.

MARTIN. Always.

KARIN. I'm sure I will want you again, one day. It's not that I don't want you, I don't know.

MARTIN. It could be anything.

KARIN. Does it worry you?

MARTIN. No. Not a bit.

KARIN. It worries me. It used to make me feel loved. I'm so tired.

She almost flops onto the bed.

Shouldn't we do something?

It isn't cold.

MARTIN. Darling.

KARIN. You need a nice wife. A big, warm, cuddly one who brings coffee and buttered toast to you in bed. Who gives you children. A flower, a big open flower for you to pollinate, as often as you like.

MARTIN. Karin.

KARIN. I'm sorry. I want you to be happy.

MARTIN. It's you I love.

KARIN. I know. I do. But you could do better.

MARTIN. I don't want anyone else. I want you just the way you are.

KARIN. That's just it with you. You say all the right words but they're still wrong somehow. How is that?

Dad can write down terrible words but you… you are worse. It's what's behind your words. How can you be so wrong?

MARTIN. If I do the wrong thing, it's out of love. That, you should at least take into consideration.

KARIN. Anyone who really loves would always do the right thing by the person he loves.

MARTIN. Then you don't love me?

KARIN *does not respond.*

I'm going with David to town to get supplies, I'll see you this afternoon.

Scene Nine

MAX *is alone with his school books, but he is looking at a pornographic magazine. He is transfixed by the pictures, one hand on his groin.* KARIN *sneaks in behind him and grabs the magazine away from him. He snatches at it desperately but can't get it. She is laughing at him.*

MAX. Give it back. What the hell is so funny?

KARIN *is stunned by his fury. She hands him back the magazine, he grabs it and rolls it up tight.*

Well? What?

Silence.

Go on then. Have a good look.

He tosses her the magazine. She flicks through it idly, stopping every now and then to take in the elaborate combinations and positions.

KARIN. They're very… athletic.

MAX. What? They're just pictures, everybody at school looks at them. What?

KARIN. Which is your favourite?

MAX. I don't know.

I don't really look at them, that much.

KARIN. Don't be such a prude. I like this one.

KARIN *shows him a page.*

She seems genuinely very enthusiastic.

And popular.

MAX *points to another picture.*

MAX. She looks soft.

KARIN. Is she the one you imagine when you write your plays?

MAX. Shut up.

KARIN. She looks very loving.

MAX. Fat lot of good it does me.

MAX *grabs the magazine back.*

Stop it, it's mine. It's mine and it's private.

It's mine, to help me masturbate. Don't you understand?

KARIN. Are you going to hit me?

MAX *spits at her.*

I'm sorry. It's my fault, I shouldn't be so nosy.

MAX. I can't talk to you! How can you understand what I'm feeling? I can't talk to you. I can't talk.

KARIN. It's all right. It's not bad. Maxie? Maxie?

She hugs him and soothes him.

All right? All right? Forgive me. It was mean and silly.

MAX. I don't know what's wrong with me. I don't want to, but then suddenly I'm so full of these feelings.

KARIN. How's your homework? Dad wanted me to make sure you worked while they were in town. Have you finished?

MAX. Nearly.

KARIN. Want to show me?

MAX. Okay.

MAX *flicks through the homework on the table. He shuts it.*

Do you ever feel… shut inside yourself?

KARIN *picks up* MAX*'s schoolwork.*

Karin?

KARIN. What?

MAX. Shut in. You've got your stuff, I've got mine. It's like I'm in a box. Each of us, Dad too, especially Dad.

KARIN. No.

MAX. Then it's just me.

KARIN. It's hot.

She puts the books down and lies back.

MAX. How did you sleep? I hardly slept.

KARIN. When you lie back, if you stare for a long time, everything can seem really scary.

MAX. Scary?

KARIN. Like it's a different world you're looking at. Scary but tempting.

Do you think I'm just ill as well?

MAX. I don't even think you are ill. I think you're bored. I think you and Martin are so boring that you just want to make yourself more interesting.

KARIN *laughs.*

What do you actually do all day? What do you do?

KARIN. I'm on my own in the house a lot when Martin is at work, but I don't mind. I don't get bored.

MAX. I don't see there's anything wrong with you.

Quiet.

KARIN. What do you remember about Mummy?

MAX. Not much.

KARIN. Do you remember the time we did the nets in the middle of the night?

MAX. No.

KARIN. You fell and banged your head.

MAX. I don't remember that.

KARIN. You were very small and there was a lot of blood. And when we got back, I remember the look on Dad's face. Like he might just run away from us. And I thought, he doesn't understand Mummy, poor Daddy, he just doesn't understand the game.

MAX. You used to say she was a princess. After she'd gone.

KARIN. I'd forgotten that.

KARIN *smiles at the memory; she makes a decision.*

Maxie, something incredible is happening to me.

MAX. What?

You can tell me.

KARIN. I want to. It's been so hard not saying something that you're thinking about every moment. But I know we can talk and the others won't mind.

MAX. Who? Dad?

KARIN. Oh no. You can't say anything to Dad and especially not Martin. I've tried to talk to them and it's no good.

MAX. Who won't mind then?

KARIN. If you want to talk, don't get all idiotic with questions. There's only so much I'm allowed to tell you. If that isn't enough for you then I won't be able to tell you at all.

MAX. Okay. You can trust me.

She stands up suddenly.

KARIN. I'll show you.

She takes his hand. The sounds of a thunderstorm in the distance.

Scene Ten

MARTIN *and* DAVID *are on their way back in the boat.*

Silence.

DAVID. What's your problem?

MARTIN. Me?

DAVID. You've been like this all morning. In town. What is it? What have I done now?

MARTIN. I can't tell if there's any point talking to you at all. I mean, I've already tried to get you to look after your daughter.

DAVID *cuts the engine. The boat slows to drifting.*

DAVID. What?

MARTIN. Karin…

DAVID. Yes.

MARTIN. She went through your desk this morning. She read your diary.

What was in it?

DAVID. Well, you tell me.

MARTIN. She told me to ask you. It was about her illness. About what we discussed last night. She read it and told me to ask you. What did you write in your diary?

DAVID. It's my diary –

MARTIN. David?

DAVID. I wrote that it was hopeless.

MARTIN. Which it isn't. Necessarily.

DAVID. You didn't make it sound good.

MARTIN. Anyway, she told me that much. That much is obvious. She said there was something else.

DAVID. I wrote… I'm a writer.

I wrote that I have a terrible… interest… in it. To see how… to observe its progress and her… descent.

MARTIN *is disgusted*. DAVID *is mortified*.

MARTIN. Christ.

DAVID. I'm not going to explain, there's no excuse. I can't defend myself.

MARTIN. It's always about you.

'Observe its progress and her descent.' You're so fucking frigid.

DAVID. You don't understand.

MARTIN. Oh, I understand. I understand all right.

DAVID. Do you think I'm proud of it?

MARTIN. You know what? Yes. I think you are proud of it. I think, you think this one will be great literature. This one will be critically acclaimed. Your own daughter's torment.

Her torture, her agony, her pain.

DAVID. I love her.

It doesn't change that.

MARTIN. I bet you do. Love her? What an opportunity. There's a Nobel Prize here.

DAVID. I feel for her.

MARTIN. You haven't got any feelings. You've no room for them. You know how they should be expressed. You can put words to it. But you don't know what it means to feel. You don't have a clue. And actually, actually that's what your books are like.

DAVID. What does that mean?

MARTIN. I'm sorry I asked you to just try and concentrate and do something for Karin.

DAVID. What do you want me to do? What can I do?

MARTIN. Look after your daughter.

Instead of this lazy, shallow, posturing.

Oh, just write your fucking book, go on. Pity it's going to be, you know, the usual…

MARTIN *stops himself.*

DAVID. Say it.

MARTIN. Your work is cowardly, sloppy. You carry on about God and faith and doubt but the real genius of your books is in not getting to the crux of anything valuable. You set up all this grand story but it's just empty posturing. Written for university students to discuss. There's no insight. All I hear is someone trying to sound troubled. What's really in your stories is the lengths you go to, to prove you might actually have a heart.

DAVID. Don't you think I know all this? Have for years?

What do you want me to do?

MARTIN. Stop lying. You're so goddam clever that your lies look like truth.

I want you not to make use of your daughter. I want you not to twist her suffering into your search for meaning.

DAVID. You really have no demons? No trouble controlling your innermost feelings?

MARTIN. Me? I'm a doctor. I look after people.

DAVID. But can you control your darkest thoughts?

MARTIN. I'm not as complex as you. Thank God. My world is a lot more simple and human.

DAVID. You've never wished Karin was dead?

MARTIN. What? Don't try and force me into one of your idiotic plots.

DAVID. I'm not saying you really wanted it but have you never had the thought? It would seem understandable to me.

MARTIN. Understandable?

DAVID. You know her illness is… awful. She's not going to recover. There's no sense in the suffering. She would be better off dead.

MARTIN. This is gross. You are gross.

DAVID. All I'm saying is that it's possible you might have thought it.

MARTIN. This is meaningless.

DAVID. No. We're all fallible.

MARTIN. I love Karin and I can't do anything. Only stand at her side and watch as she is tormented. I can't help her.

I don't wish her dead, David, I wish her alive again.

Do you know, she won't even admit that she is sick any more. At least we used to be able to talk about it. Agree that the illness was dreadful. Now she says she finally feels useful!

And do you know what I think? I think if you had ever actually been there for her, ever actually been present in her life, she might not need to retreat somewhere in search of purpose.

Even I'm useless now. She turns away from me at every opportunity. Sometimes I think she even possibly hates me.

DAVID. There's a reason she married you.

MARTIN. What does that mean?

DAVID. You were kind.

I haven't been a father to her.

To either of them.

The irony is that I came here this summer to make things better.

MARTIN. Don't you always?

DAVID. No. Not at all.

I've been running away from my children for as long as I can remember.

MARTIN. Don't tell me you had an epiphany.

DAVID. It turns out it's not so easy to change. I haven't been able to make anything better. Families are locked into a way of being together.

And now it seems, from what you've said, that if anything I've made things worse.

MARTIN. So it's hard, try harder.

DAVID. Convince myself of my good intentions. Like you do? I can go through the motions. It only means you don't have to think about the shit piling up while you look the other way.

MARTIN. At least I try.

DAVID. You try what you try.

MARTIN. And what? You write books?

Which is worth more than a person's suffering?

DAVID. No! Nothing is worth more or less. My attempts are just not the same as yours.

MARTIN. Of course! I'm trying to help Karin, you're seeking the divine!

DAVID. I'm not seeking… I've been looking for meaning –

MARTIN. Oh God –

DAVID. – my whole life.

Isn't everyone?

And, yes, yes, I come up short. Constantly. Unbearably.

It became so bad in Switzerland that I was certain I would kill myself. I'm not looking for sympathy. These last few months, I thought I could just quietly, privately… an end to the agonising. And honestly, the thought was just a massive fucking relief to me.

MARTIN. Well, that's brilliant, David, that's exactly what your daughter needs. And just out of interest, what is a quiet suicide exactly? What does that look like?

DAVID. You're missing the point. I'm still here! Here I am! Not because I couldn't go through with it or out of any grudging sense of duty –

MARTIN. What has this to do with Karin?

DAVID. The more I thought about it, planned it, took solace in it, the more I began to feel something else.

Love. For Karin, for Maxie, for you.

Meaning.

Silence.

I'm going to try to stop running away. I can't really explain it any better.

He starts the motor of the boat.

Scene Eleven

They are in the derelict room.

KARIN. I went through this wall.

MAX *is watching her closely.*

I don't know how. I heard whispering early this morning; they were calling me. I got up and I came here to this room. I had this incredible feeling inside me. A hollow feeling of longing, incredible longing waiting to be filled. People called to me from behind the wallpaper. I went to the wall and pressed through it like feathers until I was inside.

I was inside.

MAX. Where, Karin?

KARIN. You think I'm just talking.

She runs her hand along the wall to the crack.

But this entrance, it's for me, it's just for me.

It's a big room. It's so lovely and we are all waiting. If you just let the light in, your face is warm. And I am important in this room, they've told me that. He'll come when I'm there. The door will open and the faces will all turn towards Him.

MAX. Who?

KARIN. No one says, not definitely, but you know, you can tell, that it will be God. And they're just waiting for me to decide to stay in the room because I am special. And they don't mind waiting because it feels so good to hope. It feels so glorious to have this sweet anticipation, like fingertips all over your skin. Like warm wind. All of us are calm and it's so gentle. And the love… the room is full of love. The love they feel for me, these bright shining people. I am adored, I am their hope.

KARIN *speaks in more hushed tones. She weeps.*

I can bear my guilt. We're strong. You're strong.

MAX. Why guilt, have you done something bad?

KARIN. I have.

I have lied to Martin. He's too weak to hear the truth. He wouldn't understand. So I pretend that I still belong here with him. But he says such stupid things which make me angry, and then there's the guilt because I'm keeping him in the dark.

But I can't stay here just to keep Martin happy or to make Dad feel better.

I think I have to go.

MAX. Go where?

KARIN. Can't you see? I'm trapped in the middle here, between things. And I know what you're thinking: you're thinking it can't be true. But when I was in hospital having treatment, it was like dreams. Martin calls them episodes. The voices came but then I would sort of wake up from it. This is not like dreams, I'm awake when it happens and they tell me to come here. So this is real. The things I feel when I'm in there are better than any other feelings I've ever had.

It must be real.

MAX. But not to me. Karin, I'm telling you, it's not real to me.

She strokes the wall.

KARIN. I'm not dreaming, it's the truth. There are two worlds and I have to choose. Why would I not go where I am most needed?

They've told me to let go of Martin.

A moment of realisation.

And I have. I have let go of him.

MAX. Should we go for a swim?

I'm going to.

Karin?

KARIN. What were we talking about?

I'm sleepy.

KARIN *lies down on the floor.*

MAX. Karin?

KARIN. Go away. I need a rest and some quiet. Go away.

MAX *heads towards the door. Before he makes it,* KARIN *has jumped up and grabbed him from behind.*

Did you finish your comprehension?

Shocked, MAX *nods.*

Let's go through it together. Should we go through it?

Do you want tea?

Are you going to tell?

MAX. Who?

KARIN. Martin. Dad.

MAX. Tell them what?

KARIN. Cunning, but you can't fool me.

I've seen what people are like, all smiles and wide eyes, then they take Martin aside and, 'oh, I've got such and such to tell you about Karin' and they spill the beans.

MAX. Can't you tell him yourself? It's not for me to say. Probably you should, but I won't.

KARIN. Promise?

MAX. I said, didn't I?

KARIN. You understand, I feel that. But if you say anything, even hint, then you've deceived me.

There is a crack of thunder. KARIN *grabs* MAX.

I'm so lonely. Martin makes me feel so alone. I say awful things. They tell me to do things I don't want to do. I'm so confused.

The sound of rain. Drumming around and pouring down on an old roof.

The rain is here.

KARIN *is holding onto* MAX. *She hears whispering.*

MAX. Karin?

She drops to her knees and brings him down with her.

Karin?

KARIN. They're coming.

MAX. Karin, it's me. Max.

She pulls him in to a kiss.

Karin, is that you? It's me.

KARIN. You have to help me. You have to help me.

He kisses her back and then suddenly tries to scrabble away. She pulls him to her and presses herself on him. At first MAX *resists but soon they are rolling together. The rain is drumming around them and streaming through the window.*

Scene Twelve

The sound of rain builds and builds. And suddenly stops. Silence except for the dripping of gutters and the trickle of water.

MAX *is sitting on the floor, his sick sister in his arms. Around them are the pages of* MAX*'s play, which have fallen from his back pocket.* MAX*'s eyes are open and he is staring out.* KARIN*'s eyes are closed.*

MARTIN *and* DAVID *are standing, looking at them.* MAX *suddenly becomes aware of them.*

MAX. I don't know what happened, she was terrified, I didn't know what to do!

MARTIN. Karin?

KARIN *is strangely calm.*

KARIN. What time is it?

MARTIN. What happened here?

KARIN. I've been dreadfully ill. I'm better now.

She looks at MAX.

Oh God, poor Maxie.

MARTIN *moves towards her.*

I want to talk to Dad. Alone.

MARTIN. I need to get you out of here.

KARIN. Let me talk to my father before it starts again.

MARTIN. Karin, please.

MAX. You heard her.

MARTIN. Stay out of it.

KARIN (*to* MAX). It's okay.

MAX. She's my sister.

MARTIN. Quite.

KARIN. Martin!

MAX *runs out of the room.*

MARTIN. If they would just keep out of it you could be better.

KARIN. Don't pick on Maxie.

I won't be long, Martin, please, while I'm still calm.

MARTIN. All right.

Stay with your father. I'm going to ring for an ambulance.

KARIN *nods.* MARTIN *goes.* DAVID *moves from his place in the doorway.*

KARIN. What time is it?

DAVID. Four.

KARIN. It rained. Didn't it?

DAVID. Yes.

KARIN. I have that feeling like I've been crying for hours. It's hard to breathe.

DAVID. We should –

KARIN. No. I need you to listen to me.

DAVID. Yes.

KARIN. I want to stay in hospital. I've made up my mind.

DAVID. Why would you want to go back to hospital?

KARIN. I'm frightened, I don't feel in control. I've tried to look after you all, but I can't do it. I've made my choice. In hospital there won't be any confusion about any of you.

DAVID. In hospital they'll treat you.

KARIN. You have to tell them not to. The treatment confuses me. It's perfectly simple, I won't be any trouble. Can you explain that to them?

DAVID. I don't think it works like that.

KARIN. It's living between two worlds. You must know I can't do that. I've made my choice. You have to let me go.

DAVID. We'll see what we can do. Be calm.

KARIN. Not we. You. You have to help me now.

I can't stand it any more.

DAVID. What?

KARIN. The badness.

KARIN *is beginning to break. What follows is the worst of it for her.*

DAVID. What badness?

KARIN. The voices tell me to do bad things that I don't understand. But I have to do them.

DAVID. Like reading my diary.

KARIN. Yes. I didn't want to.

DAVID. I know.

KARIN. And now I've done something worse than that. Much worse.

DAVID. I see.

KARIN. I tried not to. Poor Maxie.

DAVID. I'll talk to him. Try to be calm.

KARIN. There's no way back now. Do you see? After what I've done, I have to go.

And really I'm lucky. What I have.

My room. Where everybody's waiting.

DAVID. Go on.

KARIN. The bright ones will wait till the door opens. God will come. They say that I can make it happen. And I am ready. I know that I have a thing inside me that is better than anything I actually do when I'm here with all of you. I know you understand what I'm talking about, like Maxie does.

If there was a place you could go to, where that better part of you could live, you would go, wouldn't you?

DAVID *nods.*

Who's to say which is the dream? It feels real to be there and it feels better. I can't use words like you would, but when I'm not there it's like I'm suffering a loss. I ache to go back.

But then the voices come and tell me to do things. And all my certainty goes and I get confused again and I can't make sense of it.

I wonder then, is this because I'm ill? Or is it just because I'm torn between worlds? I see my own confusion… and it's terrifying.

I know it's not as bad for me as for some people. Those poor people in the hospital. And the screaming.

I know I'm not like that but what scares me is the confusion, that's when I'm dangerous.

It's over; she's told him the worst of it. She sits silently.

DAVID. I want to ask you to forgive me.

KARIN. You've had your work.

DAVID. The suffering I've allowed to happen in the name of my work.

KARIN. I read what you wrote about Mummy.

And this is DAVID*'s worst.*

DAVID. When she got ill I went away and left you with Granny. I couldn't bear to see it happen to her, and of course I had my novel. My perfect excuse. Then she died and I had my big success. And I was relieved.

But I did love your mother, in my own selfish way.

KARIN. Am I like her?

DAVID. So like her.

KARIN. When I got ill, you went to Switzerland.

DAVID. I couldn't watch you inherit the illness. So I ran. After all, I had my novel to finish.

KARIN. Will it be good?

DAVID *doesn't answer. He shakes his head, and reaches out for* KARIN.

DAVID. The way I see it, you draw a magic circle around yourself and throw out anything you don't like. And then along comes life, to smash up your circle and show you what a fool you are. So then what do you do? Draw another circle and start again.

KARIN. Poor Dad.

DAVID. Yes, poor Dad, he'll have to live in reality one day.

But do you understand what I'm telling you?

KARIN. We better go now.

DAVID. You can't just throw out the things you don't like.

KARIN (*ignoring him*). Don't blame Maxie. Don't blame anyone, but especially not Maxie. Please?

DAVID. Okay.

KARIN. Look after him, I've hurt him.

DAVID. Yes.

KARIN. I have to pack.

MARTIN *comes in quietly with his doctor's bag*.

You've got your bag.

DAVID. She's all right.

KARIN. I'm quite calm. Thank you, I'm fine.

(*To* MARTIN.) Help me pack, will you. I'm so tired.

(*To* DAVID.) What a pity we won't be able to go mushrooming together.

KARIN *is suddenly distracted and drawn back to the crack in the wall.*

MARTIN. Come on.

But she begins talking lightly and animatedly as if DAVID *and* MARTIN *are not even in the room.*

KARIN. I know it won't be long now, it's so good to know that. Waiting has been a joy, even waiting is a joy.

MARTIN. Karin, keep calm. I'm going to give you something now.

MARTIN *moves in but* DAVID *holds him back.*

DAVID (*whispers*). Wait.

KARIN. Martin! Move softly.

They say He is coming any moment now.

Close the door.

DAVID *closes the door.*

MARTIN. Karin.

KARIN. Shh.

MARTIN. The ambulance is coming. Do you remember? We're leaving.

KARIN. I can't go now. What are you thinking?

MARTIN. Karin. No. You're imagining things.

There isn't anybody coming.

(*To* DAVID.) This is how it starts.

KARIN. Please. They've said so. I must be here.

DAVID. She seems to be fine.

MARTIN. She may be fine now –

KARIN. Be quiet! Be softly. If you can't keep quiet you should go away.

MARTIN. Karin, dear. Come along now.

Suddenly, KARIN *is furious.*

KARIN. You have to spoil everything. You have to take everything and show us all where to sit. Go away. Just for once, let us who love be with Him.

MARTIN *steps back, exhausted.* DAVID *stands quietly to the side.* KARIN *looks towards the crack in the wall. She drops to her knees.*

They say He's here. They say He's in the next room. They can hear His voice.

Martin, forgive me for being so nasty. But it's important. Can you kneel? Please. Even if you don't believe, can't you do it for me? Please.

MARTIN *kneels,* DAVID *stands and watches from the door.* KARIN *is radiant,* MARTIN *destroyed. The three of them wait in silence.*

A low growl begins, softly at first, causing KARIN*'s expression to change. Quickly, the sound is overpowering, throbbing around them: it is the helicopter ambulance.* MARTIN *stands, relieved.* MAX *comes in.*

MAX. The ambulance is landing.

But the noise has terrified KARIN. *She begins to scream.*

KARIN. Make it stop, make it stop. It's spoiling everything.

Her hands cover her ears, trying to stop the noise. Hysterical now, she throws herself into MARTIN, *who tries to hold her but she tears herself away.*

No! No! Don't say it. It isn't true. It isn't.

KARIN *looks frantically around for refuge and flings herself into a corner. She's lost any concern for her own safety. What she hears in her head is horrific.*

MARTIN *gets a needle from his bag and goes to inject her, but* KARIN *kicks out at him. He can't hold her and inject her at the same time. She's still screaming.*

Stop! Stop it!

MARTIN. David, please, she's terrified.

MAX *is waiting to see what his father will do.* DAVID *stares at his daughter.*

For God's sake, help me!

DAVID *goes to help, followed by* MAX. KARIN *continues to kick and scream as* MAX *and* DAVID *try to hold her still.*

KARIN. Daddy!

DAVID. I'm here. I'm here.

KARIN. It's horrible.

DAVID. It's all right.

MARTIN *administers the sedative and* KARIN, *who has been arching, screaming and struggling like an animal against them, gradually softens and calms.*

KARIN. I was suddenly frightened. They said such terrible things.

DAVID. It's fine now.

MAX *and* DAVID *have let her go.* MARTIN *is still holding on.*

She's not your prisoner.

MARTIN *looks appalled.*

MARTIN. What?

DAVID. Just let her go.

Karin?

KARIN. I'm okay. I'm all right. Thirsty.

DAVID *looks at* MAX, *who jumps up and runs out.*

I'm not worthy. That's what they told me. They said I was monstrous.

I've failed.

I don't know how to love.

MARTIN. That's not true.

KARIN. The door is closed to me.

KARIN *looks at the crack in the wall and then turns her head away and closes her eyes.*

DAVID *and* MARTIN, *one on each side of* KARIN, *look at each other.* MAX *returns with a glass of water which he gives to* DAVID, *who passes it to* KARIN.

MAX. They're waiting at the jetty.

DAVID. No rush.

KARIN. I'm ready.

MARTIN *and* DAVID *lift* KARIN *to her feet.*

DAVID. I'll come soon.

KARIN. I'll have to start again. I'll have to go back to the beginning and prove myself. However long it takes.

KARIN *kisses her father, smiles and then leaves, supported by* MARTIN, *without looking at* MAX. MAX, *not knowing what to do with himself, picks up the empty glass from the floor and goes after them.*

DAVID *stares at the crack in the wall, then he looks down at the pages on the floor. He picks one up, sees what it is and looks as if he might cry. He screws the piece of paper up and throws it into the corner of the room. Then he pauses, gathers himself and slowly begins to collect the pages from the floor. The sound of the helicopter taking off accompanies him.*

MAX *enters. They stare at each other in silence.*

MAX. Daddy, I need to tell you –

DAVID. Not yet.

MAX. I'm scared.

DAVID. I know.

MAX. While I was lying here on the floor… while I was…

There is deep uncertainty about how much either will say about what happened between MAX *and* KARIN.

…with Karin here… waiting for you, something happened. The world changed. Does that make sense?

DAVID. Yes.

MAX. It's never going to go back.

DAVID. No.

MAX. Am I losing my mind?

DAVID. No.

MAX. How do you live with it?

DAVID. You learn.

MAX. I don't feel safe any more.

DAVID. You find something to hold on to.

MAX. What? A god that terrifies you?

DAVID. No! Karin isn't terrified of her god. She's terrified of herself, of her own failings.

That's what'll keep her from reaching her god.

You're not worthy of happiness so you prevent it.

MAX. What do I hold on to, Dad?

DAVID. I think… I think, love.

Quiet.

MAX. Well, I'm not capable of…

I don't have the right kind of love.

DAVID. All love. The highest and the lowest, the most ridiculous and the most sublime.

MAX. The longing for love?

DAVID. That too.

MAX. And this helps?

DAVID. I don't know. I can only tell you what I think. I'm starting to see my love for Karin, and you, and our life as something practical.

A kind of pardon.

MAX. Can it help Karin?

DAVID. I hope so.

MAX. Can we talk about how to help her? Can it be something we do together?

DAVID. It can, Max.

MAX *nods.*

Blackout.

The End.